"DEDICATED TO THE DESIRE TO REACH OUT TO FAMILIES WITH A PERSONA THAT CHILDREN CAN ASSOCIATE WITH AND RELATE TO. LEARNING AND EDUCATION IS FOR EVERYONE, AND WE STRIVE FOR THAT IN THIS BOOK AND THE SERIES TO COME."

— SPIKE JARRELL

I WANNA DEDICATE THIS BOOK TO MY SON MICAIAH AND MY DAUGHTER MADELEINE. MY SON WAS THE FIRST PERSON I PITCHED THE BENNY BOOK IDEA TO AND HE ABSOLUTELY LOVED IT. HE WOULD ASK ME EVERYDAY HOW'S THE BENNY BOOK COMING ALONG? ONCE MY SIX YEAR OLD DAUGHTER BEGAN VIRTUAL SCHOOLING THIS YEAR, I KNEW I NEEDED HELP. IT WAS AT THIS TIME I REALLY BEGAN TO TAKE THE BENNY BOOK SERIOUS. SHE WOULD ALWAYS COME TO ME WITH IDEAS ABOUT THE BOOK, SOME GOOD, SOME NOT SO GOOD; BUT IT HAS BEEN ENCOURAGING TO SAY THE LEAST TO HAVE THEM BOTH SHOW SUCH INTEREST IN THE BOOK. FOR THAT I AM FOREVER GRATEFUL.

— THANX GUYS, LOVE DAD.

MY COUSIN BENNY LEARNING BOOKS SERIES IS COPYRIGHT 2020 THE KUT MAGAZINE & PAT VEGAS. ARTWORK PROVIDED BY LARRY SPIKE JARRELL AND BRASS RING COMICS STUDIOS. ANY LIKENESS TO PERSONS LIVING OR OTHERWISE IS PURELY COINCENDENTAL. MATERIALS PRESENTED WITHIN ARE FOR AGES 3-6 AS LEARNING/EDUCATIONAL. PRINTED IN THE USA BY COMIX WELL SPRING.

"Hi guys, I'm your COUSIN BENNY. I love to count. Counting is easy and it's fun. Don't worry if you don't know how to count, I'll teach you. It's as easy as 1...2...3. I hope you're as excited as I am. Let's get started!"

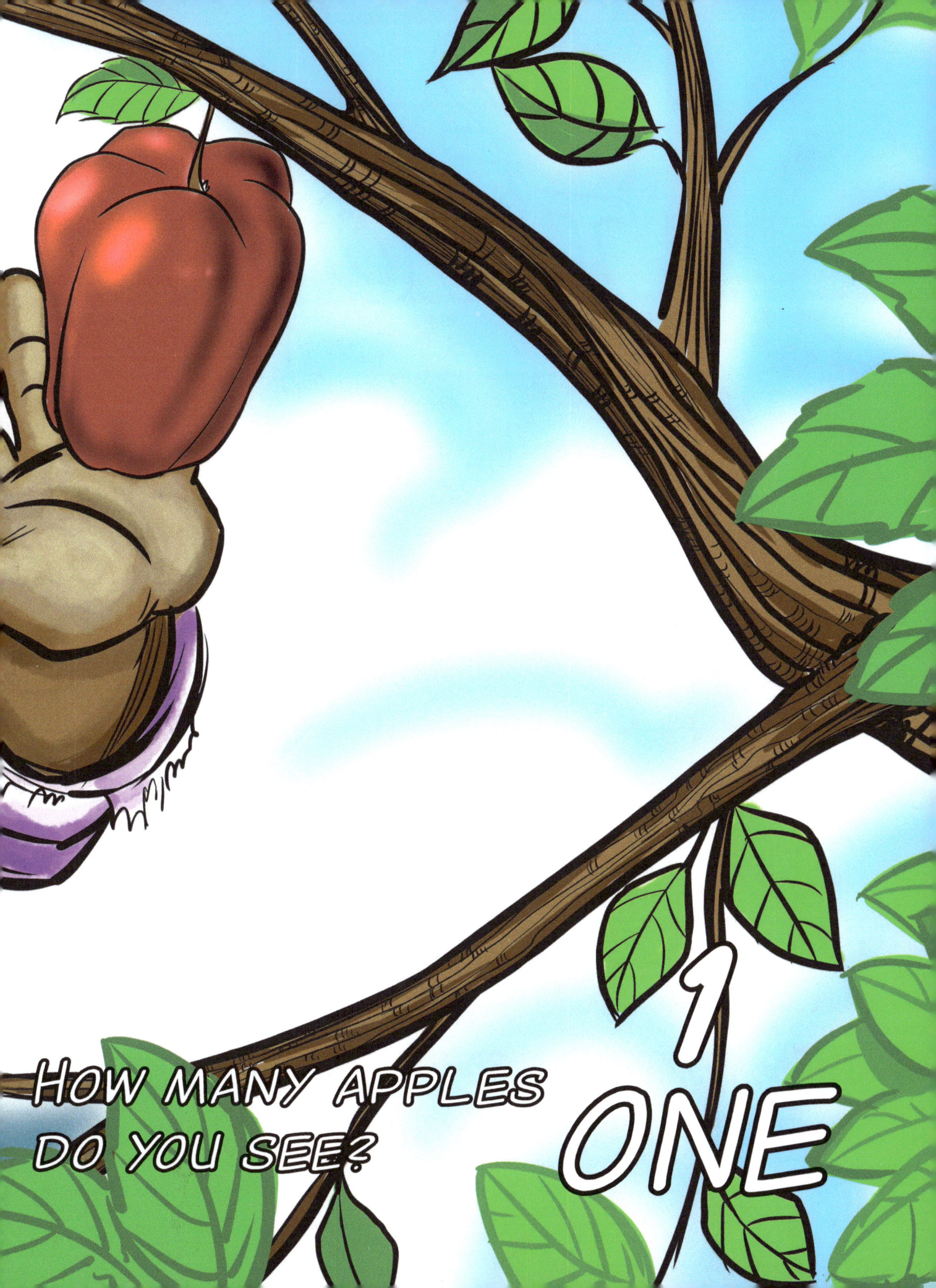

2 TWO

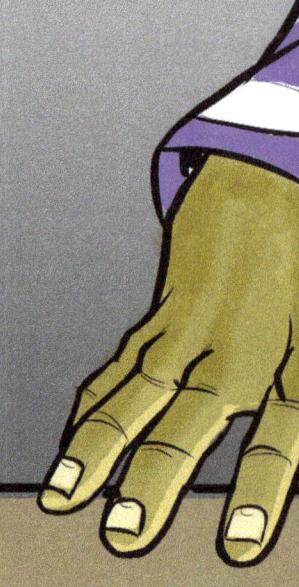

I love to color. My favorite two colors are red and blue.

How many coloring crayons do you see?

I love to play marbles.
Today I won seven marbles.

Can you count the marbles?

7
SEVEN

Oh what a surprise! Today when I got home from school my dog Bessie had eight puppies.

Let's count the puppies together.

8 EIGHT

My favorite time of the day is snack time.
I have ten doughnuts.
Would you like to have one?

Let's count the doughnuts together.

MY COUSIN BENNY LEARNING BOOKS are dedicated to making learning fun and easy. Our books are designed to help with Early Childhood Education.
Around the ages of 3-6, a child's brain is like a sponge, soaking up tons of information. Our goal is that every book helps to boost a child's confidence and knowledge, therefore leading to a better and more productive learning experience.

MY_COUSIN_BENNY

MY COUSIN BENNY LEARNING BOOKS

www.ingramcontent.com/pod-product-compliance
Lightning Source LLC
Chambersburg PA
CBHW061751290426
44108CB00028B/2960